FIRST EDITION

I0112226

GET
WRITE
ON IT

YOUR WRITING COMPANION

BY KATHLEEN D. TRESEMER

COPYRIGHT © 2024 | KATHLEEN D. TRESEMER
CONTENT COMPILED FOR PUBLICATION BY
RICHARD MAYERS OF *BURTON MAYERS BOOKS* 2024
ALL RIGHTS RESERVED.

A CIP catalogue record for this book is available from the British Library
ISBN: 9781917224031

A NOTE FROM THE AUTHOR

Hooray for writers! We all need a pal to turn to when writing gets tough, to brainstorm an idea, or you simply want to share thoughts with another writer, someone who understands.

That's why I created *Your Writing Companion*.

As a new author, I was surprised by the need to connect with others. I had been writing for years without a lot of support. I had friends, sure, but writing was alien to them. I thought I was weird, er . . . I mean, *delightfully unique*.

A diverse career helped. I wrote lots of reports working in child welfare and early education. Later I created web content for an international firm & marketing materials for local businesses. I developed a weekly newspaper column titled "The Second Half" and wrote articles and periodic features for regional newspapers and magazines. I enjoyed my success but was unsure how to write my novel.

As co-founder of In **Print Professional Writers Organization**, I was asked many questions by new and struggling writers. Not having a writing network might be the most challenging obstacle for writers everywhere.

As I gained writing friends, I learned more about options for writing. For fun, I decided to submit to a short story contest. Surprise! I earned a top ten award in the Writer's Digest 76th Annual Competition that year, with a certificate and a small check. I was elated! And that got me started toward publishing fiction.

A NOTE FROM THE AUTHOR

With my writing colleagues, I've led numerous workshops including "The Benefits of Critique" at UW-Madison Writers' Institute and "First Page: Engage!" at the Southwest Wisconsin Book Festival. Through In Print, we created years of workshops and programming to support professional writers throughout the Midwest.

Eventually, I published my first novel Time in a Bottle with Soul Fire Press, an imprint of Christopher Matthews Publishing. Most recently, I published A Case of Peaches with Burton Mayers Books, the first in a series of "social mysteries" from the files of Adoption Specialist, June Hunter.

Support can mean the difference between publishing or giving up. Thinking about what writers need was my inspiration. Your Writing Companion will be there for you, encouraging, informing, and cheering you on to the completion of your book.

Believe in Yourself!

Kathleen D. Tresemer,

TABLE OF CONTENTS

I will be beside you for the entire book, story, article, or poem you're preparing to write. I'm here for you until you complete this project. Let's get started!

CHAPTER ONE

SELF RESPECT

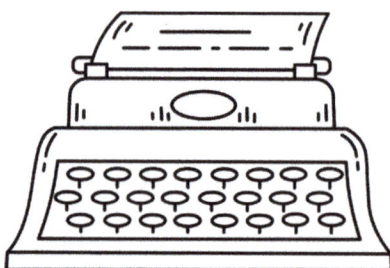

AM I A WRITER?

The first time you formed words on a page, you became a writer.
No, it isn't silly or a waste of time. Yes, some people don't understand.

Writing is one of the fine arts that has, for centuries, contributed to the richness and beauty of cultures worldwide. Society imposes negative judgements on the arts, due to the immeasurable nature of it and its subjective financial value. Fight the urge to buy into such negativity. You write because you want to. You have something to say and you are courageous enough to share it.

Anytime you find yourself shrinking from your identity, repeat out loud: *"I am a writer! I love to write! Writing is a cornerstone of culture. I am a writer and I contribute to the beauty and richness of life."*

Or just smile and remember that writing is cool!

PRO TIP:
Practice your writing self-esteem by nonchalantly telling positive recipients (e.g., teachers, librarians, and other writers),*"Yeah, I'm working on my novel today!"*

ASK YOURSELF :

- What do the negative voices (real or in my head) say about my writing?

- How do I combat those voices?

- How do I demonstrate my commitment to being a writer?

TOOLS THAT SHOW RESPECT FOR YOUR ART FORM

Every artist or craftsman requires tools. What are the tools of a writer?

- **Computer** – laptop, tablet, smart phone, vintage typewriter, etc.
- **Pens** – fountain, rollerball, gel, different colors, etc.
- **Pencils** – charcoal, #2, colored, etc.
- **Paper** – notebook, journal, legal pad, etc.

These are only a few options for basic writing. Figure out what tools you need and assemble them. For example, maybe you want to try writing out poems with a fountain pen. Go out and get a quality pen with a nib designed for smooth writing.

Don't say, "I'll just get this cheap one first and try it; if I like it, I'll buy a better one." You may not like the cheap one, and it won't really give you the experience of writing regularly with a quality fountain pen.

If you don't know which laptop will meet your needs, go to a store and try them out.Talk to computer geeks. Ask other writers. Search "best laptops for writers."

Take your writing seriously! Obtain quality tools, even if you must scrimp and save.

PRO TIP: Ask for help getting your tools from friends or family. For birthdays, holidays, and special occasions, request gift cards for those tools you consider an extravagance. "I'm writing more and more these days and saving to get a laptop from xxx store. I would really appreciate a gift card!"

ASK YOURSELF :
What tools do I want or need for this new writing venture?

What is my plan to obtain those tools?

SPACE THAT RESPECTS YOUR WRITING

Where is the best place to write on a regular basis?

Some of us like to write at home. Ages ago, I wrote at the library or coffee shop where I could submit my articles by using their high-speed internet. Later, I repurposed a small bedroom for my office. I painted it a color I loved, decorated it for inspiration, brought in a couple of bookcases, and polished up an old antique desk. It was a space that made me feel happy and motivated.

I understand William Kent Krueger wrote all his novels at a coffee shop near his home. He got up at 5:30 to go there, drink coffee, and write longhand in wire-bound notebooks. Stephen King wrote his novel Carrie in a laundry closet. It doesn't matter where, but you deserve to carve out a space that is yours for writing – just for writing, if possible.

It's hard to get serious or in a rhythm when you have interruptions or distractions. Don't get me wrong, people do it. But if you want to be productive, a designated writing space free from constant interruptions really makes a difference.

PRO TIP: If the only opportunity to write is in a crowded gymnasium during your kid's marching band practice, or something equally raucous, noise-cancelling headphones or earbuds are a great tool!

ASK YOURSELF :

- Define the space where you will be writing most of the time. Why is it the best place to work on your current project?

- How will you make this space your own?

- What is an alternate space you will use as your back-up if your space becomes unavailable?

DEVELOP A SYSTEM

We all have a system but not all systems help us succeed. If your system is "write when I feel the muse," you may never finish this project.

Consistency is the best predictor of success. Even if you can only write on the weekends, set a schedule for writing every weekend. We are creatures of habit, after all.

A system for a person who is available daily might look like this: Weekdays get up at 7:00 am, meditate, grab coffee, and write for two hours; take a shower and eat breakfast, write for three hours; weekends and holidays write 1500 words in the afternoon.

A system for someone with a full-time job and kids might look like this: write during lunch hour in the conference room; after dinner each night, write one more page; weekends, write a minimum of 1000 words daily during nap-time.

Tailor the system for optimum success (meaning it's both doable and likely you can make it work) and adjust it as you learn what works best for you. You can do this!

OUTLINE MY SYSTEM HERE :

○ _____

○ _____

DATES & CHANGES TO MY SYSTEM :

○ _____

○ _____

SET GOALS

Setting goals is the best way to help you feel prepared for this writing project and to keep you going until you finish. Goals don't have to be hard and fast, but something to strive for each time you sit down to write.

THEE ARE THREE TYPICAL GOALS

1 **Word Count :** this can change from day to day, depending upon your time and project.

2 **Time :** e.g., number of days a week, hours each writing day, or a date to complete a chapter or section.

3 **Section/Chapter :** e.g., a chapter each time you sit or a section an hour.

Hemingway wrote daily at sunrise, Vonnegut woke at 5:30, writing in two-hour intervals, and Henry Miller had a set of Commandments that ended with "write first and always."

Your goals can change. One week you might have a lot of outside interference (e.g.,midterm exams, OT at work, sick kids/spouse) or holidays to plan. Another week, you may be able to write every day without fail.

Review your goals weekly in written form using a planner, notebook, or calendar. Of course, there is space for you to flesh out these goals here.

Plot your goals before the days and weeks fill up with obligations, then fill in appointments around that. Make corrections for things such as doctor visits or a holiday concert at your kid's school. Set goals that are doable but will challenge you. Be consistent. You have the right to make your writing goals a priority.

Review your goal each time you sit down to write and each time you end a writing session for the day, so you know where you stand. Always be ready to raise the bar, because your writing gets faster and easier the more you practice!

SET GOALS

MY WRITING GOALS /DATE :

- ○ _____
- ○ _____
- ○ _____
- ○ _____
- ○ _____
- ○ _____
- ○ _____
- ○ _____
- ○ _____
- ○ _____

DATES & CHANGES TO MY SYSTEM :

- ○ _____
- ○ _____
- ○ _____
- ○ _____
- ○ _____
- ○ _____
- ○ _____
- ○ _____
- ○ _____
- ○ _____

ONLINE WRITING TOOLS

It is the Age of Wonders for online tools! While you don't need them to be a successful writer, you may find one that enhances your writing and offers feedback you like.

Below are only a few examples of online tools to explore. Decide for yourself if you'd like to try them. While some offer a free version or a free trial, be prepared to part with some cash for the premium tools.

As you discover other options, take a few minutes to research them and make notes in the spaces below. Remember, if a tool slows you down or seems very complicated, it can interfere with your main priority – to write!

Scrivener : provides manuscript organization, outlining, and more.

Pros _____

Cons _____

Hemingway Editor : assists in paring down writing using color-coded highlights.

Pros _____

Cons _____

AutoCrit : holds your manuscript to your genre's standards and is tailored specifically to fiction.

Pros _____

Cons _____

ProWritingAid : grammar checker, style editor, and writing mentor.

Pros _____

Cons _____

ONLINE WRITING TOOLS

As you search online or talk to others about their choices in writing tools, take a look at their websites. See if this might be a tool you'd like to try and write your comments below.

Other Online Writing Tools:

What's Provided

Pros

Cons

CHAPTER TWO

TIME

COMMIT TO TIME MANAGEMENT

In any project, structuring your time is the best way to be successful. It helps to avoid procrastination, empowers you against interruptions, and offers a positive space for you to practice your artform.

Many beginners write "when they can." Life's obstacles can derail this type of writer, causing frustration and stress. Successful writers make writing a priority in their lives by committing to time management and respecting the schedule.

Does guilt ("I shouldn't take away from family time") or insecurity ("I can't possibly commit to a schedule") or even fear ("What if I can't do it?") stop you from managing your time? Or do you allow the outside world (phone/social media/friends) distract you from your goals?

LET'S EXPLORE

Am I a successful time manager in other areas of my life?
List those areas.

_____

What keeps me from managing my writing time in a more effective way?

_____

What are some solutions to those things listed above?

_____

AFFIRMATIONS I LIKE FOR TIME MANAGEMENT :

- My writing has value.
- I deserve the time to create through my writing.
- Everything has its own time; this is my time for writing.
- I respect myself when I take the time to write.
- Writing fills me up so I have more to give to others.

CREATE YOUR OWN AFFIRMATIONS BELOW

○ _____

○ _____

○ _____

○ _____

○ _____

○ _____

○ _____

○ _____

○ _____

○ _____

WEEKLY SCHEDULE

If you aren't sure how to start, pick up a calendar or a piece of paper. Begin with next week.

First, list the days of the week. See what obligations you have each day. Fill these times in with pen or marker including work, caring for children, and doctor appointments, as well as travel time.

Next, fill in health activities such as eating, sleeping, laundry day, and exercising, as well as occasional and organized activities like book club, church, or volunteering.

Finally, list any social activities that occur on a weekly basis. Friday night after work with friends or visit parents for Wednesday dinner.

Now, take a look, study it.

When do you see blocks of time?

You might see Monday through Thursday after dinner is a two-hour block while the kids do homework. Maybe those weekday afternoons you fill with "miscellaneous stuff" could be used for writing. If you're determined, you will find time most days.

Find your blocks of time and schedule "Writing." Be specific and measurable (e.g., "Writing, 2:00-4:00, Monday – Thursday"). Fill in these times, putting them in your phone as appointments and set notifications.

Finally, if you find a problem (e.g., I don't get home from class until 2:00 so I started 30 minutes late every day this week), change the time to 2:30-4:30 for the next week.

Within weeks, you'll be setting a schedule that works for you!

NEXT WEEK'S WRITING SCHEDULE:

Monday

Tuesday

Wednesday

Thursday

Friday

Saturday

Sunday

CONFLICTS TO ADDRESS:

Schedule changes for rare occasions
(holidays, vacation/travel, school break, work conference, etc.)

_____

_____

_____

_____

MAKE-UP DAYS

We all get sick or have occasional appointments that interfere with our writing goals. That's why you create Make-Up Days. In my writing group, we write together 2 days a month. We pick a time that works for all of us and commit to a certain schedule.

For example: meet at 9:00 a.m., eat breakfast, write from 10:00 a.m. – 2:00 p.m. We always let the restaurant staff know we will be taking up space for a few hours and tip accordingly.

Make-Up Days don't have to be this formal. You may decide that a certain day each month is a catch-up from life's inconveniences. I've taken days at the library, coffee shop, or friend's house. Writing days with others have a different energy that motivates and inspires me.

It doesn't matter how you schedule these days. Build in a block of time to write like crazy. I feel better knowing I have built in days that are just for me and my muse.

ASK YOURSELF:

When can I schedule a special writing day?

Date: _____

Can I find a day once a week/month/season?

Date: _____

How did my recent Make-Up Day enhance my writing?

_____

_____

_____

_____

SOCIAL MEDIA

You know social media can be a real time suck!

Most seasoned writers deliberately break from social media during certain times of the day. Time spent responding to texts or chats while you write does not meet your writing goal. Social media is not your priority.

Turn off notifications, put your phone in another room, do whatever it takes to avoid these obvious interruptions.

Schedule social media time for after you meet your daily writing goal, as a reward. Set a timer to let you know when to stop being social and get back to work.

Managing time is about predicting those things that get in the way of successfully meeting your priorities

ASK YOURSELF :

Does social media have a place in my life?

How much time do I spend on social media? When do I spend the most time?

How will I control my social media usage, so it won't interfere with my writing goals?

_____

_____

_____

_____

CHAPTER THREE

RESEARCH

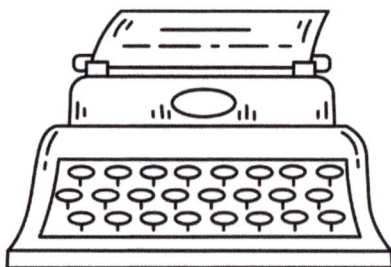

GENRE

There are 5 main genres of literature:
Fiction, Drama, Poetry, Prose, and Non-Fiction.

You may write in different genres such as Fiction and Poetry. You may write in one genre but different sub-genres such as YA Fiction and Historical Fiction. Whatever your writing forms, you must identify your genre and discover the rules of your work.

For example, Romance is a Fiction sub-genre with a few clear-cut rules:

1. It must have a happy ending HEA or "happily ever after";
2. Developing a relationship is the most important part;
3. Subplots must be resolved along with the HEA;
4. Tropes are acceptable, expected, and loved by the readers;
5. Know your audience expectations for the type (historical, young adult, erotic, etc.).

The best way to learn what the expectations are for your genre is to READ, READ, READ! Schedule reading time as part of your research. Read on the subway, at lunchtime, before bed . . . whatever works for you.

Plan to read in the genres you write but try to diversify as well. I never thought I would write YA Fiction until I read my neighbor's favorites. I deliberately explore all genres for the exposure and inspiration. I also go to the library and talk to the staff, getting the latest info on newer offerings in different genres.

ASK YOURSELF :

- What is the Genre/Sub-Genre for this project:

- What are the "rules" for this genre?

- How does my writing measure up against the standards for this genre? Where do I need to change/improve?

TRAINING

As in any occupation, continued improvement and skill development are critical to our growth as writers. No one becomes a better writer by hiding your head in the sand.

Options for training are abundant, from basic writing classes to workshops in publishing and sales. Most writers I know take regular training in their craft very seriously.

One way to do this is by taking classes. There are many options for classes: local colleges and universities; online training; writing organizations; and conferences/workshops.

Schedule training regularly! A writing group in my area organizes a trip to a conference or workshop each year. They look for a keynote speaker that writes in a genre they enjoy and offers classes with qualified trainers such as successful authors and professors. We all attend together. We plan to get the most out of all the classes, discussing our experiences and copying/sharing handouts.

ASK YOURSELF:

- In what area would I like to have training this year?

- Options for obtaining such training?

- What did I attend/read/participate in; how did it help me?

EVENTS

Author events are abundant in most communities and range from author signings/readings to writing retreats. Attending some type of writer's event each quarter helps to provide outside stimulus and networking opportunities. I still get giddy meeting a famous author or poet and always take away something to enrich my writing!

Look for events through a variety of different sources, such as:

- Libraries
- Bookstores
- Colleges & Universities
- Writer Organizations
- Author Websites
- Publisher Websites
- Writer's Digest/Writing Magazines
- Community Event Calendars
- Coffee Shops/Wine Bars

Attending these events has many benefits, the least of which is meeting like-minded people to build your writing community.
Writing friends are the BEST!

ASK YOURSELF :

- What are some desirable writing events coming up?

- List events attended & notes about strengths/weaknesses.

HOW-TO STUFF

Walk into any bookstore and marvel at the selection of "How to Write" books available. An Internet search for sites that tell you "how to write..." offers unending options.

I have a variety of books on my shelf, from Stephen King's "On Writing" to Anne Lamott's "Bird by Bird." These books vary from technical to inspirational.

If you like that sort of thing, go for it; if not, you do you. Remember to schedule time for that outside of your writing. Don't let learning "How To" keep you from DOING!

ASK YOURSELF :

- What types of "How To" stuff do I look at?

- Does it improve my writing or help me procrastinate?

- What "How To" tools could help me improve right now?

- What "How To" tools have I explored during this period of writing (be specific) and what was the result?

ANYTHING ELSE?

Resources can mean anything from pencils to setting reminders on your Alexa.

As you come across options, list them here and then investigate.

Just because your other writing friends jump off a bridge, does that mean you need to as well?

> **"** ─────────────
>
> Write, my companion, just write!
>
> ───────────── **"**

ASK YOURSELF :

- What will this item do for me?

- Does it improve my writing in some way?

CHAPTER FOUR

SUPPORT

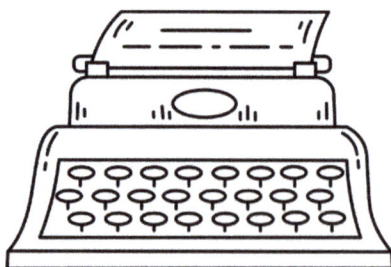

WRITING GROUPS/ORGANIZATIONS

I highly recommend writing groups and organizations as a terrific place to find support!

Organizations fulfill multiple needs for a writer. An example is the Chicago Writers Association (www.chicagowrites.org). They offer members a blog, writing groups, reviews, conferences, contests, and a speaker's bureau.
A simple online search will help you locate such organizations.

Writing Groups are another animal entirely. They seldom have an online presence and can be difficult to locate. My writing groups were all informal, discovered by word-of-mouth or private invitation.

Some groups discuss writing, some are for networking, some offer critiques, and some gather to sit and write - period. Locating the right group can take time and legwork.

My writing groups are an important part of my life and a priority.
I currently attend three: one for networking with other authors, one for feedback, and one intensive group that supports my complete writing practice.

ASK YOURSELF :

- To what Writing Organizations or Groups do I belong? How are each serving me?

- Am I looking for more? Where have I looked?
  (name/email/website/phone)

- How many writing friends have I made recently? Where will I go to meet others?

CONFERENCES/RETREATS

Conferences and Retreats can provide workshops, speakers, and other opportunities to hone your craft. While it isn't necessary to attend expensive programs, most will cost more than a hamburger and fries.

The educational opportunity at such an event is exciting. Be certain to verify that the conference supports your interest, needs, and genre to get the most for your money. Some are geared for specific writers (mystery writers, for example) while others are "something for everyone" affairs.

Most conferences offer writing contests. Submit to these contests. You may get some good feedback. And you might win!

I recommend attending with friends - it's a lot more fun. You may want to travel together or share a room to assist with cost. Some even have scholarships that will cover part of the expense. Any way you do it, you'll take something away that helps or inspires you and you'll likely meet some new friends.

ASK YOURSELF :

- What Conferences/Retreats appeal to me?

- How will I pay for the conference/room/meals/travel? Will I need financial help (any scholarships or discounts)?

- Do I know anyone who might like to join me?

- Book it! Dates and registration:

SOCIAL MEDIA

I belong to author groups on Facebook and Instagram, so I can be honest with you. Social Media Author Groups are abundant. Problems facing those groups: marketers flooding members with advertisements or offers to publish, scam artists preying on a captive audience. That almost put me off those groups for good.

Be alert to these issues and remember: an in-person group or a virtual group is less prone to scammers. However, with some searching, you can find a great group on social media that supports your writing journey.

As we've discussed previously, social media can suck the time out of a day. Even a writer's group that's helpful and inspiring can lead down a rabbit hole of endless clicking. The group should support your writing, not take time away from it. Try restricting your participation to specific time frames and set an alarm.

All groups will have some rules posted. Read them prior to joining a group to be certain of a good fit.

Remember, any group requires some participation.
Be prepared to give back.

ASK YOURSELF :

- Do I want to participate in an online group?

- What groups look promising?

- Am I willing to give as much as I get from the group?

- How will I keep from getting lost in social media?

LIBRARIES/BOOKSTORES

Author events at libraries and bookstores are a great way to meet other writers. I know, standing with a bunch of introverted writers you don't know can be uncomfortable at first. Not a lot of us want to initiate contact, right?

Try interacting by saying something bland to no one in particular: "What a cool event!" Any person who answers is probably willing to engage. Then you can ask, "Are you a writer/author/poet?" or "Do you know the guy who'll be reading?" That should get the ball rolling.

The people who run indie bookstores are a great resource. They know tons of authors and may make introductions. They can steer you to book clubs, open mic events, and book signings. They like to carry local author books so make that connection whenever possible.

Librarians can be good resources too. My librarians share all kinds of "writerly" info and will let me know about new local authors. My library hosted my book launch party for "A Case of Peaches" and it was a smashing success. I can't live without my library fix every week or two!

In addition, many libraries and bookstores have Events Boards where author events are posted. Even if you post a bookmark for your recent novel or your author business card, you are still getting your name out there.

ASK YOURSELF :

- Am I getting out to bookstores and libraries and introducing myself? Which ones?

- Have I enquired about Book Clubs, Local Author Signings, and other events?

- List those I have not yet visited and schedule a date and time to go – ask a friend to join you.

CHAPTER FIVE

JOY

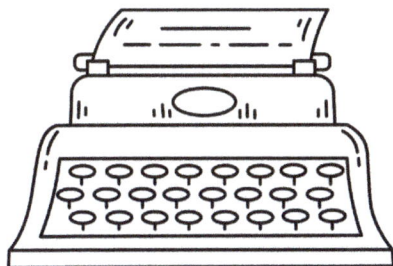

WHAT'S SO GREAT ABOUT WRITING?

I'm Your Writing Companion, here to help keep the joy in your writing process during difficult times. Each writer is different, so a bit of reflection is in order.

A dip in the joy can come at different places in my novels. I tend to get one in the middle of the novel, when the resolution/conclusion is far off, and I find my energy lagging.

It isn't just once either. Everyone has times that frustrate them, times when you'd like to give up. Don't. Turn to this page and remind yourself that writing is something you love!

Why do you write? It's a personal and elusive question. Finding the joy can be more of a journey than a destination, so let's get to it.

ASK YOURSELF :

- Why did I start writing?

- What do I dislike about writing?

- What do I love about writing?

- Times I've needed to remind myself about the joy during this project (date/place in the process)?

today
I CHOOSE
joy

MEDITATION

A little bit of meditation can do a lot for my writing. If you haven't tried it, trust me. Learning to turn off all the noise so you can focus on your writing is a skill that can only help.

I tend to visit YouTube for my meditations. I like to listen to ambient music and focus on my breathing, saying "I am" on the in-breath and "a powerful writer" on the out-breath. Different variations of this affirmative meditation include: "I love...my characters." "My writing...feeds my soul." "I am...a successful author." "I am...a writing rock star."

You can make up more to fit your own style.
Some days, all I can say is "I am . . . a writer."

Guided meditations to support writers are available in abundance. Most are short, about 5-10 minutes. They can be fun and helpful; I recommend trying them.

Search YouTube with "meditations for writers" and find enough options for two lifetimes. They are designed for empowerment, focus, creativity, developing your characters, etc. Pick one and listen. Try it for two weeks before you write, then decide if it works for you.

Walking meditation is another variation. Like breathing affirmations, try using them to your steps, slowly left foot then right: "My writing . . . brings me joy."

ASK YOURSELF :

- Am I willing to try meditation to improve my writing and bring me joy?

- List meditation types with dates/feelings about it.

SELF-SOOTHING

As Your Writing Companion, I am a firm believer in feeling good while I'm writing. Listen to music, eat junk food, or light candles, whatever makes it nicer is worth doing. Go nuts!

While music, candles, and eating are typical, there are a variety of things that make sitting down to write a true pleasure. Special furniture to enhance comfort is an absolute must! We addressed furniture in Section I, Self-Respect. I say, "Nothing brings me more joy than a beautiful desk and supportive chair."

There are as many ways to self-soothe as there are writers.

Some ways include:

- Wear comfy or special clothing (e.g., an old sweater)
- Essential oils to diffuse or rub on your skin
- Crystals or rocks in your writing space
- Totems of turtles (creativity), eagles (vision), or others
- Plants in your writing space
- Certain colors surrounding you
- Rubbing textured items or worry stones
- Positive Affirmations

ASK YOURSELF :

- How do I self-soothe? Does it add joy to my writing practice?

- Is there something special I want, to improve my joy? When/how will I get it?

- Do I self-soothe in harmful ways (e.g., overeating or drinking)?

- What would be a good replacement for those harmful ways?

NATURE

Take a break to walk in nature! It's a great way to enjoy your writing life and calm negative thoughts. I like to sit on my patio or deck and feel the sun on my face. Birds make me happy too, both watching and listening to them.

However, going outside isn't always feasible. I live in the Midwest where snow, ice, and wind are prevalent.

There are other ways to enjoy nature outside. One is to sit by a window and enjoy the weather from inside. There's nothing so stimulating or joyful than watching a thunderstorm or blizzard from a safe space. Or consider listening to sounds of nature such as a rainstorm, birds chirping, or a babbling brook.

Bring nature inside by creating a desktop garden, fragrant herb pots, a terrarium, or even a bonsai tree. While these options require some care, it can be a joy to work on them.

ASK YOURSELF :

- Do I enjoy nature on a regular basis?

- What ways to enjoy nature appeal to me?

- How can I integrate nature into my writing life to bring me joy?

WHAT ELSE BRINGS ME JOY?

Sometimes we forget the things that bring us joy: swinging at the playground, riding a bicycle, baking cookies, etc.

List below the things that bring joy to your life and think about adding them into your writing routine.

After all, JOY is what it's all about!

ASK YOURSELF :

What brings me joy?

-
-
-
-
-
-
-

CHAPTER SIX

PROMPTS

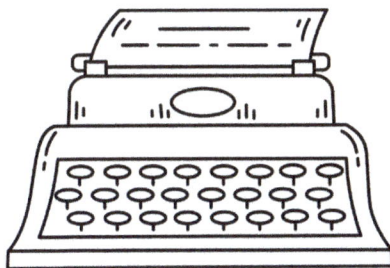

HOW TO USE PROMPTS

Writing prompts are popular because they get your brain in the creative space.

You don't need to pay for prompts unless there's a book of them that really speaks to you. Simply search "creative writing prompts" and lots of websites offer them for free (e.g., writersdigest.com). Pick one that looks fun or inspirational and write to a set goal (time or word count).

You can make up your own prompts too. Pick a character (yours or any character from books/tv/movies) and put them in a funny or unique place.

Find a selection of prompts on the *next few pages*.

DOROTHY FROM THE WIZARD OF OZ
Writing Prompt

Describe your favorite female romance character's day from the POV of an elderly man who walks with a cane.

FORETELLING
Writing Prompt

Write a scene from Santa Claus' childhood that foretells his future as "toymaker for the world."

_____

_____

_____

_____

_____

_____

_____

_____

_____

_____

_____

_____

_____

_____

_____

_____

_____

_____

_____

_____

_____

_____

_____

_____

PICK A LOCATION

Choose a character from a book you enjoy. Write a scene
introducing that character living in a different location
(e.g., a fisherman introduced as a guy in a Las Vegas casino).

PROMPTS FOR DIFFERENT THINGS
Point of View

Pick a favorite scene from your current WIP and
write it in a minor character's POV.

_____

_____

_____

_____

_____

_____

_____

_____

_____

_____

_____

_____

_____

_____

_____

_____

_____

PROMPTS FOR DIFFERENT THINGS

Point of View

Write the first scene of a mystery novel from the point of view of a parrot.

_____

_____

_____

_____

_____

_____

_____

_____

_____

_____

_____

_____

_____

_____

_____

_____

_____

_____

_____

_____

_____

_____

PROMPTS FOR DIFFERENT THINGS

Point of View

Pick a scene from a book you've read and write yourself into it in your POV.

_____

_____

_____

_____

_____

_____

_____

_____

_____

_____

_____

_____

_____

_____

_____

_____

_____

PROMPTS : LOCATION

Write the first three paragraphs of a mystery story in your locale and then write it set in Antarctica.

_____

_____

_____

_____

_____

_____

_____

_____

_____

_____

_____

_____

_____

_____

_____

_____

_____

_____

_____

_____

PROMPTS : LOCATION

Pick an exotic (to you) location you have always imagined you would visit and describe it in 250 words.

_____

_____

_____

_____

_____

_____

_____

_____

_____

_____

_____

_____

_____

_____

_____

_____

_____

_____

_____

_____

PROMPTS : LOCATION

Develop a character who lives on a mountain:
describe his first visit to town.

_____

_____

_____

_____

_____

_____

_____

_____

_____

_____

_____

_____

_____

_____

_____

_____

_____

_____

_____

PROMPTS : THE SENSES

Describe music to a deaf child approximately 10 years old.

_____

_____

_____

_____

_____

_____

_____

_____

_____

_____

_____

_____

_____

_____

_____

_____

_____

_____

PROMPTS : THE SENSES

Pick three herbs/spices; describe how they
smell in an unusual way.

_____

_____

_____

_____

_____

_____

_____

_____

_____

_____

_____

_____

_____

_____

_____

_____

_____

_____

_____

_____

PROMPTS : THE SENSES

Explain what the Wicked Witch saw from the tornado as Dorothy spies her out of the window (from Wizard of Oz movie).

_____

_____

_____

_____

_____

_____

_____

_____

_____

_____

_____

_____

_____

_____

_____

_____

_____

_____

_____

_____

PROMPTS : THE SENSES

Write three paragraphs describing the taste of honey
from a honeybee's POV.

_____

_____

_____

_____

_____

_____

_____

_____

_____

_____

_____

_____

_____

_____

_____

_____

_____

_____

_____

_____

_____

_____

_____

PROMPTS : THE SENSES

From the POV of a woman trapped in the trunk of a car, describe everything; then write the same from a male POV.

_____

_____

_____

_____

_____

_____

_____

_____

_____

_____

_____

_____

_____

_____

_____

_____

_____

_____

_____

_____

PROMPTS : CHARACTER BUILDING

From a favorite character's POV, explain a strength they wish they had.

_____

_____

_____

_____

_____

_____

_____

_____

_____

_____

_____

_____

_____

_____

_____

_____

_____

_____

_____

PROMPTS : CHARACTER BUILDING

Pick a character from a book and add a character flaw that makes sense.

_____

_____

_____

_____

_____

_____

_____

_____

_____

_____

_____

_____

_____

_____

_____

_____

_____

_____

_____

PROMPTS : CHARACTER BUILDING

Describe how a hero feels when one of his flaws is unkindly revealed by a good friend.

_____

_____

_____

_____

_____

_____

_____

_____

_____

_____

_____

_____

_____

_____

_____

_____

_____

_____

_____

_____

_____

PROMPTS : CHARACTER BUILDING

Write 250 words describing how Mickey Mouse learned to find happiness.

_____

_____

_____

_____

_____

_____

_____

_____

_____

_____

_____

_____

_____

_____

_____

_____

_____

_____

_____

_____

_____

PROMPTS : SET UP A MYSTERY

Describe the location of a murder at night, and then during the day.

_____

_____

_____

_____

_____

_____

_____

_____

_____

_____

_____

_____

_____

_____

_____

_____

_____

_____

_____

_____

PROMPTS : SET UP A MYSTERY

Pick a silly or funny location for a murder; describe in the scariest way you can.

_____

_____

_____

_____

_____

_____

_____

_____

_____

_____

_____

_____

_____

_____

_____

_____

_____

_____

_____

_____

PROMPTS : SET UP A MYSTERY

"It was a dark and stormy night when Snoopy wandered into the dog food store…" Then what?

_____

_____

_____

_____

_____

_____

_____

_____

_____

_____

_____

_____

_____

_____

_____

_____

_____

_____

_____

_____

PROMPTS : THE BEST & WORST

Describe the best thing Sherlock Holmes discovered at the scene of a gruesome murder.

_____

_____

_____

_____

_____

_____

_____

_____

_____

_____

_____

_____

_____

_____

_____

_____

_____

_____

_____

PROMPTS : THE BEST & WORST

Write a worst- case scenario for sulky teenager on Christmas Eve.

_____

_____

_____

_____

_____

_____

_____

_____

_____

_____

_____

_____

_____

_____

_____

_____

_____

_____

_____

_____

_____

_____

PROMPTS : THE BEST & WORST

A terrorist threatens to detonate a bomb containing deadly gas at a busy airport; create a scene for each of the best and worst possible scenarios.

CHAPTER SEVEN

WRITERS BLOCK

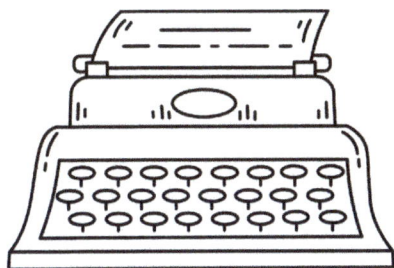

DEFINE WRITER'S BLOCK

Wikipedia calls it a non-medical condition, primarily associated with writing, in which an author is either unable to produce new work or experiences a creative slowdown. Hmmm... that sounds horrifying.

A crippling case of writer's block, one that prevents you from successfully producing the pieces you want on a continuing basis, may necessitate professional help. And, if that's the case, go for it! Therapy is a gift to yourself, so embrace it!

This section is for the occasional rough patch or dry spell many writers experience during the course of creating.

I prefer to setup my life so that WB can't sneak in. It helps tremendously to write on a schedule. Good habits regarding time management, research, attitude, and support are the best defense against writer's block.

Meditation works well for me. It helps quiet the mind. Ten or fifteen minutes of meditation each day prior to beginning your writing is easy to add to your schedule. If you don't know how, search "how to meditate for beginners" and learn.

A SIMPLE WALKING MEDITATION GOES LIKE THIS:

- Choose a path through your house or yard

- Set your phone timer for ten or fifteen minutes

- Slowly breath in on step one and out on step two, repeating continuously as you walk the path

- When the timer goes off stop, take a deep breath in, slowly let it out, get yourself a nice drink of water, and return to your writing.

DEFINE WRITER'S BLOCK

Take a break for creativity. Sometimes a cup of coffee or a handful of chocolate helps. Turn to Section VI. and work through a few prompts. I don't recommend alcohol or other mind-altering substances.

You probably can't walk into your boss's office and refuse to work, no matter how you feel. Your writing is your work, too. Give it the importance it deserves; don't give WB a chance.

Finally, try some of the Pro-Tips on the following pages.

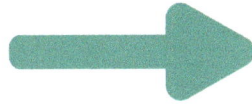

PEN & PAPER

Switch to pen/pencil and paper for writing. Create an outline or draw a diagram to demonstrate what happens in your troubling section. Make a visual representation of how to get there.

Describe your experience.

_____

_____

_____

_____

_____

_____

_____

_____

_____

_____

_____

_____

_____

_____

_____

SWITCH IT UP

Getting stuck on a chapter or section can be rough. Make a switch; start writing another part (e.g., your introduction to your book). Or have a character look around and describe an object or scene to write into your story. The more unlikely a scene, the more fun it can be. Maybe it's snowing in the desert!

Describe your experience.

_____

_____

_____

_____

_____

_____

_____

_____

_____

_____

_____

_____

_____

_____

BRAINSTORM

Make a list of possibilities, such as "the worst thing that could happen to my character" or "crazy ways to end this section." Set the timer for 10-15 minutes. List ideas until the timer goes off!

Describe your experience.

_____

_____

_____

_____

_____

_____

_____

_____

_____

_____

_____

_____

_____

_____

_____

_____

CALL A FRIEND

Text a writing pal with this message: "Got a minute to brainstorm?" If they say no or don't respond in a few minutes, repeat with another writing pal. When you get on the phone, NO SOCIALIZING! Only talk about what's troubling you and see if they have another perspective.

Describe your experience.

_____

_____

_____

_____

_____

_____

_____

_____

_____

_____

_____

_____

_____

_____

_____

_____

REVIEW YOUR ENVIRONMENT

See if you can identify any new distractions and eliminate them. Use all of your senses. Write down things that could be distracting and solutions to those problems.

Some ways to improve your environment are to turn on a lamp or put a cushion on your chair. Take off your shoes or put on your favorite sweatshirt. Light a candle or rub on essential oils.

Describe your experience.

TAKE A BREAK

Sometimes all we need is a little nurturing! Get yourself a cup of coffee or tea. Eat some chocolate.

Light a scented candle or diffuse some essential oils. At the very least, take a bathroom break, wash your face, put on lotion, brush your hair. Write these things down so you can reflect on them later: did they help?

Always remember to see about H.A.L.T.
Are you:
- **H**ungry?
- **A**ngry or frustrated?
- **L**onely?
- **T**ired?

Describe your experience.

_____

_____

_____

_____

_____

_____

_____

_____

_____

_____

EXERCISE

Take a walk, do some stretches, turn on music and dance.
Record what works and keep those helpful things in your arsenal.

Describe your experience.

_____

_____

_____

_____

_____

_____

_____

_____

_____

_____

_____

_____

_____

_____

"WHAT IF" GAME

When you get stuck, it's always fun to play the "what if" game. What if your character fell and banged his head? What if the urban character woke up in a hammock on a tropical beach? What if you added a truly ornery cat to your main character's life?

You may not use the "what ifs" you come up with, but it will get those juices flowing!

Describe your experience.

_____

_____

_____

_____

_____

_____

_____

_____

_____

_____

_____

_____

_____

_____

BUTT IN SEAT

Sit down and write. Set a timer or a word count goal and write. Don't stop until you hit the goal. Jodi Picoult is a prolific author. Her motto is, "you can't edit a blank page." Write, write, write!

Describe your experience.

_____

_____

_____

_____

_____

_____

_____

_____

_____

_____

_____

_____

_____

_____

CHAPTER EIGHT

QUOTES & AFFIRMATIONS

GET INSPIRED!

Seeking inspiration from positive affirmations and quotes will help you put things into perspective. I use them on a regular basis to keep my head in the game, especially when writing a long piece like a novel.

Find quotes/affirmations that speak to you on the following pages.

Each day, write your thoughts down and add new ideas.

You are worth it!

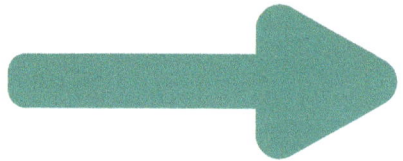

WRITE LIKE IT MATTERS, AND IT WILL.
- Libba Bray

DESCRIPTION BEGINS IN THE WRITER'S IMAGINATION, BUT SHOULD FINISH IN THE READER'S. - Stephen King

WRITING IS THINKING. TO WRITE WELL IS TO THINK CLEARLY. THAT'S WHY IT'S SO HARD.

- David McCullough

EITHER WRITE SOMETHING WORTH READING OR DO SOMETHING WORTH WRITING.

- Benjamin Franklin

TRY TO WRITE A BOOK YOU BELIEVE THAT ONLY YOU CAN WRITE. - Daniel Loedel

---

A WRITER'S JOB IS TO TELL THE TRUTH.

- Andy Rooney

A PROFESSIONAL IS AN AMATEUR WHO DIDN'T QUIT. - Richard Bach

_____

_____

_____

_____

_____

_____

_____

_____

_____

_____

_____

_____

_____

_____

_____

_____

_____

🙶 MY WRITING INSPIRES ME.

_____

_____

_____

_____

_____

_____

_____

_____

_____

_____

_____

_____

_____

I AM PROUD OF MY ABILITY TO CRAFT A STORY.

I AM CREATIVE AND PERSISTENT IN MY WRITING.

I FINISH WHAT I START WITH LITTLE EFFORT.

THE BEST WAY TO FINISH A BOOK IS TO BEGIN WRITING.

IF I BELIEVE IN MYSELF, ANYTHING IS POSSIBLE.

❞ I ENJOY SITTING DOWN TO WRITE.

_____

_____

_____

_____

_____

_____

_____

_____

_____

_____

_____

_____

_____

_____

> WRITING FEEDS MY SOUL THE WAY
> CHOCOLATE FEEDS MY DESIRE.

WRITING IS INTOXICATING.
I ENJOY EVERY WORD.

_____

_____

_____

_____

_____

_____

_____

_____

_____

_____

_____

_____

_____

_____

_____

TODAY I ENCOURAGE MYSELF TO KEEP WRITING.

WHEN I SIT AT MY COMPUTER, NOTHING CAN STOP ME FROM WRITING!

I SEE MYSELF AS AN EXCEPTIONAL STORYTELLER.

_____

_____

_____

_____

_____

_____

_____

_____

_____

_____

_____

_____

_____

_____

_____

_____

I WILL ACHIEVE GREAT THINGS WITH MY WRITING.

I BELIEVE IN MYSELF AND MY WRITING.

I AM CREATIVE AND WORTHY OF RESPECT.

I KNOW WHO I AM: A WRITER.

_____

_____

_____

_____

_____

_____

_____

_____

_____

_____

_____

_____

_____

_____

_____

_____

I AM IN THE PROCESS OF A CREATIVE ADVENTURE.

_____

_____

_____

_____

_____

_____

_____

_____

_____

_____

_____

_____

_____

I BELIEVE IN MY ABILITY TO ACCOMPLISH MY WRITING GOALS.

_____

_____

_____

_____

_____

_____

_____

_____

_____

_____

_____

_____

_____

_____

_____

I AM A WRITER AND I CONTRIBUTE TO THE BEAUTY AND RICHNESS OF LIFE.

QUOTES & AFFIRMATIONS

QUOTES & AFFIRMATIONS

IF YOU'RE HERE, YOU MUST BE DONE WRITING THIS BOOK OR NOVEL.

Congratulations!

☐ What other steps do you need to take at this point?
(e.g., Hire an editor? Come up with a strategy to release your work?)

☐ Now list the places where you'll submit your work/how you want to publish.

☐ Begin your next book or novel!

_____

_____

_____

_____

_____

_____

_____

_____

_____

ABOUT THE AUTHOR

Kathleen D. Tresemer is a writer and author. She has published novels in both YA and Women's Fiction. As a founder of In Print Professional Writers Association, Kathleen has helped authors throughout the Northern Illinois and Southern Wisconsin region of the Midwestern US.

Based on her years of developing writing workshops and education for authors, **Get Write On It: Your Writing Companion** is meant to assist any author through the process of developing their writing projects.

Her published novels include:

- *Time in a Bottle*: 2016, Soul Fire Press/Christopher Matthews Publishing.
- *A Case of Peaches*: 2023, Burton Mayers Books; first in a series of "social mysteries" from the files of Adoption Specialist, June Hunter.
- Coming in 2024: *Channeling Socrates*, second in the June Hunter series.

authorkdtresemer@outlook.com

facebook.com/kathleentresemerauthor